Learn to DRAW

Fairies, Mermaids and Unicorns

Jorge Santillan and Sarah Eason

WAYLAND

First published in 2015 by Wayland
Copyright © Wayland 2015

Wayland
338 Euston Road
London NW1 3BH

Wayland Australia
Level 17/207 Kent Street
Sydney, NSW 2000

Produced for Wayland by Calcium
Design by Paul Myerscough
Illustrations by Jorge Santillan

A catalogue record for this book is available from the British Library

Dewey classification: 743.8'939821-dc23

10 9 8 7 6 5 4 3 2 1

ISBN: 978 0 7502 9091 3
eBook ISBN: 978 0 7502 9093 7

Printed in China

Wayland is a division of Hachette Children's Books,
an Hachette UK company.
www.hachette.co.uk

Contents

Learn to Draw!

Fairies, mermaids and unicorns are truly magical creatures. They can be found in many wonderful stories and pictures, and some people even say they have seen these beautiful beings in real life. We'll show you how to draw fairies, mermaids and unicorns – and if you really believe in them, perhaps you might see one in real life, too!

You will need:

Just a few simple pieces of equipment are needed to create amazing drawings of fairies, mermaids and unicorns:

Sketchpad or paper
Visit an art shop to buy good quality paper.

Pencils
You will need both fine-tipped and thick-tipped pencils.

Rubber
Don't worry if you make a mistake – use a rubber to remove any unwanted lines. You can even use it to add highlights.

Paintbrush, paints and pens
Buy a set of quality paints, brushes and colouring pens to add colour to your stunning drawings.

Forest Fairies

Have you ever heard a rustle in the woods? It may have been a bird or a bear – or perhaps a forest fairy hiding out of sight! The forest is full of pretty fairies that flit from tree to tree. So next time you take a walk in the woods, look out for fairy friends!

Step 1

Draw the fairy's body and dress. Then draw her head, arms, hands, wand, legs and feet. Draw crescents for the fairy's wings.

Step 2

Now add the fairy's hair, ears and eyes. Draw the leaf collar and the fairy's dress. Rub out the rough lines from step 1.

Step 3

Add detail to the eyes, and draw the nose and mouth. Pencil the fingers, boots, leaf bracelet and the magic twig wand. Add the antennae.

Step 4

Pencil the folds on the fairy's dress, add detail to her ears and draw the lines on her wings.

Step 5

Add shading to the fairy's dress, wings, hair and face. Don't forget to shade her arms, hands, legs and boots, too.

Step 6

Now you can start to colour your fairy. Use a dark green for the fairy's skirt, boots, leaf bracelet and leaf collar. Paint the bodice of her dress light green. Colour the wings light blue and give your fairy rich red-brown hair. This fairy has bright green eyes to match her dress!

Step 7

Bring your fairy to life with touches of white for highlights. Add highlights to the wings, hair, face, arms, legs and dress. Your cute forest fairy is now complete!

Forest Hiding Holes

Foxglove flowers grow wild in many forest places. Little forest fairies love the foxglove because it is a perfect hiding place! The pretty fairies sit inside the 'cup' of the flower – and peek out at passersby. Some people say that the foxglove flower even bends down from its stalk to say 'hello' to nearby fairies!

Water Fairies

Fairies that live in water are tiny creatures that are rarely seen. People have believed in water fairies for thousands of years. Some say they have seen fairies flitting through the water like tiny darts of light. Others claim they have seen beautiful fairies, like this pretty water fairy, flying above rivers and streams.

Step 1

Draw the fairy's body and dress. Then draw her head, arms, hands, legs and feet. Add her wings.

Step 2

Go over the lines from step 1 to draw the outline of the fairy. Rub out the rough lines you drew in step 1. Pencil the fairy's eyes, ear and hands.

Step 3

Now begin to add detail. Draw the fairy's hair and dress. Draw her fingers, then add some detail to her face and the edges of her wings.

Step 4

Now add the holes on the wings, and draw the belt, headband, bracelets and boots. Define the features of the fairy's face.

Step 5

Add further shading to the folds on the fairy's dress and her wings. Add some light shading to her face and her arms and legs.

Step 6

Now you can start to colour your fairy. Use a pretty pink for the fairy's dress. Then paint the belt brown, with a red jewel for the buckle. Colour the wings light blue and give your fairy golden hair. Use a very light pink for the fairy's skin and a light blue for her pretty eyes.

Step 7

Bring your fairy to life with touches of white to add sparkle. Dot splashes of white around the fairy's wings, hair and dress. Finish your picture by adding some highlights to the face, arms, legs, wings and hair. Your pretty water fairy is now complete!

Fun-loving Fairies

Fairies that live in water are also called 'sprites' or 'nymphs'. These fairies can swim underwater like a fish, and are full of fun. Some people say they can change their shape to look like an insect or a flower, to help them hide when people are near!

Fire Fairies

Dancing in the flames of any fire are the fire fairies. These spritely little creatures love the crackle, heat and colour of a fire. Fire fairies are full of fun – but watch out! These mischievous fairies love to play naughty tricks on anyone who might be watching them…

Step 1

Draw your fairy in a leaping pose. Draw her body and dress. Then add her arms, hands, legs, feet and wings. Add the flame.

Step 2

Mark the fairy's eyes and pencil her dress, belt and hair. Draw the edge of the flame.

Step 3

Now draw the outline of the eyes and add the nose and mouth. Draw the fingers and the edges of the wings. Draw the cross on the dress.

Step 4

Draw fiery flames at the edge of the fairy's arms and add the lines on her hair and dress.

Step 5

Now you can shade your fairy. Add shading to her dress, body, face and hair. Use shading marks to add a pattern to the wings and flame.

Step 6

Bring your fire fairy to life with colour. Use a bright orange for the fairy's hair and eyes. Now colour the skin light brown, and the dress a deep, dark brown. Use yellow for the lower arms, hands, feet, flame and the fairy's wings.

Step 7

Add a red outline to the wings, lower arms, hands, feet and the flame. Use light orange to add more shading and the pattern marks. Finally, add highlights and colour the eyeballs and teeth white.

Firework Fun

Fireworks are a fire fairy's favourite! These fairies love to watch fireworks bang and flash. They jump in and out of the colourful sparks, and zoom among the lights in the sky. The next time you watch a firework sparkle in the sky, look out for fire fairies nearby!

Beautiful Mermaids

Deep beneath the ocean waves, mermaids swim in watery caves. For hundreds of years, people have believed in mermaids. Sailors from long ago told tales of mermaids calling to them from the waves. Some even say they saw these beautiful creatures sitting on rocks to comb their hair as they sang!

Step 1

Draw the mermaid reaching up towards the ocean surface. Draw her body and long, fanned tail. Then add her head, arms and hands.

Step 2

Add the mermaid's eyes and hair and the shape of her hands.

Step 3

Now draw the star in the mermaid's hair, then add the curls of her hair, the belly button and the area where her tail joins her waist. Draw the mermaid's face and fingers, too.

Step 4

Draw the headband, necklace and bracelets. Add the pattern on the tail and the lines on its tip.

Step 5

Shade the mermaid's hair, body, arms, face and tail. Add deeper shading to the jewellery.

Step 6

Colour the tail with a beautiful blue-green shade. Use a light brown for the skin and a rich yellow for the mermaid's hair and bracelet. Then colour her necklace and headband deep red and her eyes bright blue.

Step 7

Now colour the mermaid's teeth bright white and add the whites of her eyes. Use light tints to add highlights to her tail, hair, jewellery and skin. Your watery beauty is ready to swim the seas!

Forever Young

Mermaids never grow old! They stay young and beautiful forever. They are also very strong and can swim through the ocean waters as quickly as a shark!

Powerful Unicorns

You might mistake a unicorn for a horse, but look a little closer and you'll see the amazing horn on this magical creature's head. You'll never see a unicorn by day – these powerful beasts appear only under moonlight.

Step 1

Draw the unicorn's body, neck and head. Draw the horn on the head. Then add the legs, hooves and tail.

Step 2

Pencil the mane, tail, nostrils, ears and the eye. Draw the curving lines of the unicorn's head, chest, neck and legs. Rub out the lines from step 1.

Step 3

Now add the mouth and the detail of the mane, hooves and tail.

Step 4

Draw the marks on the unicorn's horn and add detail to the eyes.

Step 5

Start to bring your magical creature to life with shading. Use light strokes to begin with, then add some heavier marks for darker areas.

Step 6

This unicorn is a beautiful pink colour. Cover the body with a light pink, then add a deeper shade on its belly, legs and under its neck. Colour the mane and tail purple and the horn brown.

Step 7

Finally, add highlights to the unicorn's mane, tail, body, horn, hooves and eye. Your graceful unicorn is now complete!

A Unicorn's Magic

Long ago, people believed that a unicorn's horn was so powerful it could cure sick people. By touching the horn of a unicorn, a person could be healed. It was even said that they might then live forever!

Flying Unicorns

Some magical unicorns have a truly incredible power – they can fly. These amazing creatures have huge wings that they use to lift them up into the air so they can soar through the sky.

Step 1

Draw the unicorn's body, neck and head. Add the horn on its head. Then draw the legs, hooves and tail. Add the wings.

Step 2

Add the curving lines of the wings, mane, legs, neck and tail. Pencil the eye and ear. Rub out the rough lines from step 1.

Step 3

Draw the feathery lines at the edge of the unicorn's wings. Add detail to the mane and tail. Draw the mouth, jaw and nostril.

Step 4

Add more detail to the wings and mane. Draw the lines on the horn and the lines on the unicorn's tail, neck and face.

Step 5

Shade your unicorn's body, neck, legs, face, mane and tail. Carefully shade the huge wings to show their feathers.

Step 6

Colour your unicorn white. Use gold for the mane and tail, cream for the wings and dark brown for the hooves and horn.

Step 7

Add white highlights to the wings, mane and tail. Also give the body and face highlights to bring out the detail in your picture. Your wonderful unicorn is ready to fly!

Unicorn King

The most famous winged unicorn is Pegasus. In Greek legends, Pegasus was a great, powerful unicorn that had many adventures. One day, the king of the Greek gods, called Zeus, turned Pegasus into many beautiful stars. If you look up into the night sky, you can see the starry shape of the unicorn!

Glossary

adventures exciting journeys or experiences

antennae the 'feelers' on top of a creature's head. Antennae help creatures to feel their way around

crescents long, curved shapes that look a little like half moons

cure to make well again

detail the fine lines on a drawing

fairies magical, flying creatures that can perform spells

features the eyes, eyebrows, nose and mouth of a face

fireworks sparkling, brightly-coloured objects that are activated when lit with a match or flame

flit to quickly fly

foxglove a brightly-coloured flower with large petals

highlights the light parts on a picture

hooves the hard parts on an animal's feet

horn a long, hard, pointed part on an creature's head

insect a creature with two wings, six legs and three parts to its body

magical to do with magic

mermaids beautiful creatures with the tail of a fish and the body and head of a woman. Mermaids live in the oceans

mischievous loves to play tricks

nostril an opening on an animal's head through which it breathes

pose the position a person or creature is in

rustle the sound that an animal or an object may make as it moves against something

sailors people who sail boats or ships

shading the dark markings on a picture

soar to fly easily through the sky

spritely full of life and energy

stalk to follow something or someone without being seen

starry lots of stars

unicorns magical creatures that look like a horse but have a horn on their heads. Some unicorns have wings and can fly

winged to have wings

For More Information

Books

Amazon Digital, *How to Draw a Unicorn In Six Easy Steps* (Kindle Edition), Amazon Digital, 2011

Daisy Meadows, *The Magical Crafts Fairies: 142: Annabelle the Drawing Fairy*, Orchard Books, 2014

Linda Ravenscroft, *The Fairy Artist's Figure Drawing Bible*, Search Press Ltd, 2009

Websites

Find out more about fairies and play lots of fun games on Disney's website at:
disney.go.com/fairies

Find out more about mermaids at:
www.thekidswindow.co.uk/News/Mermaids.htm

Read the story of *The Little Mermaid* at:
www.childrenstory.info/childrenstories/thelittlemermaid.html

Find out more about unicorns at:
www.thekidswindow.co.uk/News/Unicorns.htm

Index